D0762375

ARISTOTLE'S
DIVINE
INTELLECT

THE AQUINAS LECTURE, 2008

ARISTOTLE'S DIVINE INTELLECT

MYLES F. BURNYEAT

MARQUETTE
UNIVERSITY
PRESS

B
491
.I55
B87
2008

·i 1286299x

91009707

Under the auspices of the
Wisconsin-Alpha Chapter of Phi Sigma Tau

LIBRARY OF CONGRESS CATALOGING-IN-PUBLICATION DATA

Burnyeat, Myles.
  Aristotle's divine intellect / Myles F. Burnyeat.
    p. cm. — (The Aquinas lecture ; 2008)
  Includes bibliographical references.
    ISBN-13: 978-0-87462-175-4 (clothbound : alk. paper)
    ISBN-10: 0-87462-175-5 (clothbound : alk. paper)
  1. Aristotle. 2. Intellect. I. Title.
  B491.I55B87 2008
  128'.3—dc22

                                    2008000291

Printed in the United States of America.

♾The paper used in this publication meets the minimum requirements of the
American National Standard for Information Sciences—
Permanence of Paper for Printed Library Materials, ANSI Z39.48-1992.

Association of American
University Presses

MARQUETTE UNIVERSITY PRESS
MILWAUKEE

The Association of Jesuit University Presses

Prefatory

The Wisconsin-Alpha Chapter of Phi Sigma Tau, the International Honor Society for Philosophy at Marquette University, each year invites a scholar to deliver a lecture in honor of St. Thomas Aquinas.

The 2008 Aquinas Lecture, *Aristotle's Divine Intellect*, was delivered on Sunday, February 24, 2008, by Myles F. Burnyeat, Emeritus Fellow of All Souls College, Oxford University, and Honorary Fellow of Robinson College, Cambridge University.

Myles Burnyeat studied Classics and Philosophy at King's College, Cambridge and pursued gradu-

MYLES F. BURNYEAT

ate studies at University College, London, where he also taught from 1964-1978. In 1978 he moved to Robinson College, Cambridge University, and was appointed Laurence Professor of Ancient Philosophy there in 1984. In 1996 he was appointed Senior Research Fellow in Philosophy at All Souls College, Oxford University. He has held visiting appointments at numerous universities, including the University of Pittsburgh, Princeton University, Harvard University, University of California at Berkeley, and the Central European University in Budapest. He has given many invited lectures, including the Tanner Lectures on Human Values at Harvard University, the A.E. Taylor Lecture at University of Edinburgh, and the British Academy Master Mind Lecture.

Among other honors and awards, Prof. Burnyeat was elected a Fellow of the British Academy in 1984, was President of the Mind Association in 1987, became a member of the Institut International de Philosophie in 1988, was made a Foreign Honorary Member of the American Academy of Arts and Sciences in 1992, and was President of the Aristotelian Society in 2005-06. Most recently Prof. Burnyeat was named a Commander of the Order of the British Empire for his services to scholarship.

Prof. Burnyeat has been a prolific scholar, having published two books, *The Theaetetus of Plato* (with its 240 page introduction) and *A Map of Metaphysics Zeta*. He has edited or co-edited eight books, including *Doubt and Dogmatism*, *Science and Speculation*, and *The Skeptical Tradition*. His breadth of research interests can be grasped from the titles of a few of his publications, many of which have been translated into other languages: "Aristotle on Understanding Knowledge." "Idealism and Greek Philosophy: What Descartes Saw and Berkeley Missed," "Did the Ancient Greeks Have the Concept of Human Rights?," "Culture and Society in Plato's *Republic*," "Aquinas on 'Spiritual Change' in Perception," "Platonism in the Bible: Numenius of Apamea on *Exodus* and Eternity," ""Examples in Epistemology: Socrates, Theaetetus and G.E. Moore, "The Past in the Present: Plato as Educator of Nineteenth-Century Britain."

To Prof. Burnyeat's distinguished list of publications, Phi Sigma Tau is pleased to add: *Aristotle's Divine Intellect*.

ARISTOTLE'S
DIVINE INTELLECT

M. F. BURNYEAT

> Natural selection could only have endowed savages
> with a brain a few degrees superior to that of an ape,
> whereas he actually possesses one very little inferior to
> that of a philosopher.
>
> Alfred Russell Wallace

My title is ambiguous and I intend it in both senses. 'Aristotle's intellect' may mean the intellect Aristotle speaks of as God in *Metaphysics* Λ and as the Active Intellect in *De Anima* III 5. It may also mean the intellect that is active in Aristotle himself when he discourses on these lofty themes. My claim will be that both senses lead to the same reference. When we read *Metaphysics* Λ and *De Anima* III 5, we encounter God, the Active Intellect, explaining itself. Or so Aristotle would have us believe: when his intellect is actively explaining itself, that is his Deity explaining itself.[1]

This is of course a contentious interpretation,
but it fits well with another contentious claim, as
follows. One of the lessons we can gain from the
history of philosophy is that psychological states
are not given to us as part of the natural order. To
a considerable extent, what they are *is* how they
are conceived at this time in history or that. And
how they are conceived is not a recording of something antecedently fixed by nature, but a response
to a theoretical or - at least as often - a practical
problem. Much of what current philosophy of
mind so condescendingly calls 'folk psychology'
is the precipitate of past philosophies or religious
movements. The very concept of the mind and the
mental, as now understood, can be seen coming
to birth in the second of Descartes' *Meditations*.

I.

The earliest testimony on what 'mental' meant
before Descartes is simultaneously the first extant
occurrence of the word itself. In his *Literal Commentary on Genesis*, having set out to distinguish
tria genera visionum, three kinds of 'vision', Augustine lists and explains first the corporale genus of
vision, second the spirituale, and then says he will
call the third kind 'intellectuale ab intellectu'. So
far, nothing out of the ordinary. But suddenly he
introduces an alternative way of naming the third

kind. One might think to call it 'mentale a mente'. But no, he says, that would sound just too absurd because of the novelty of the word 'mentalis'![2]

A word that doubles for 'intellectualis' does not yet mean what 'mental' means in philosophy today. Nor does 'mens' yet mean 'mind' in our sense if it is intersubstitutable with 'intellectus'. As witness that in medieval times the two Latin nouns remain largely intersubstitutable, I can call the great thinker after whom this lecture series is named. Aquinas says, 'mens maxime dicitur intellectus': 'The mind is chiefly called the intellect'. He goes on to construct a dialectical argument which infers that *intellectus* is the subject of virtue from the premise that *mens* is the subject of virtue.[3]

Even more significant is Aquinas' quotation from Augustine a few pages earlier: 'When we come across anything that is not common to us and the beasts of the field, it is something pertaining to the mind'.[4] The old Aristotelian paradigm is still in charge. What human and other animals have in common is the power of perception. What other animals lack and humans have is the power of reason, intellect, *mens*. It follows that *mens* does not yet include perception. Enter now Descartes.

The second *Meditation*, subtitled 'The nature of the human mind'[5], leaves unchallenged the equivalence of 'mens' and 'intellectus'. Near the beginning we read, 'I am a mind or intelligence, or intellect, or reason' (AT IX 27, 13-15)[6]. Descartes can say this because he has already used the *Cogito* to deconstruct the traditional Aristotelian account of the human soul (*anima*) as responsible for nutrition, movement, perception and thought (AT IX 26, 6-8). When the body-involving elements of the ancient tradition have been doubted and removed, mind (*mens, animus*) is all that is left as essential to the Meditator. At the end of the second *Meditation* we are told that, properly speaking, it is only the intellect, not the senses or the faculty of imagination, that perceives ('percipere')[7] the wax, and it does so by understanding bodies, not by seeing or touching them (AT IX 34, 2-5).[8] In between he has worked to bring ordinary sense-perception back into his account of what he himself is, subject to the proviso that by 'perception' we are to understand the mere seeming to perceive, not veridical cognitive contact with things external to the mind:

> Lastly, it is also the same 'I' who has sensory perceptions, or is aware of bodily things as it were through the senses. For example, I am now seeing light, hearing a noise, feeling heat. But I am asleep, so all this is false. Yet I certainly *seem* to see, to hear, and to be warmed. This cannot be false; what is called 'having a sensory experience' is strictly just this, and in this restricted sense of the term it is simply thinking. (AT IX 29, 11-18; tr. Cottingham)[9]

Thus did sensory experience come to fall within the scope of the mind and philosophy of mind.

Finally, two short excerpts to confirm that Descartes was well aware that he was innovating:

> But what then am I? A thing that thinks. What is that? A thing that doubts, understands, affirms, denies, is willing, is unwilling, *and also* imagines and has sensory perceptions.[10] (AT IX 28, 20-22; tr. Cottingham)

> I am a thing that thinks: that is, a thing that doubts, affirms, denies, understands a few things, is ignorant of many things, is willing, is unwilling, *and also* which imagines and has sensory experience; for, as I have noted before, even though the objects of my sensory experience and imagination may have no existence outside me, nonetheless the modes of thinking which I refer to as cases of sensory perception and imagination, in so far as they are simply modes of thinking, do exist within me—of that I am certain.[11] (AT IX 34, 18-20; tr. Cottingham)

The italics are mine, but the punctuation comes straight from Descartes' first edition (1647), the only one to have been corrected by him.[12] In both excerpts the phrase 'and also' signals a surprise new addition to the list of items that fall under the concept of mind. In the second quotation argument is added to remind us of the justification given earlier for his novel, greatly expanded concept of mind.

In due course, even philosophers who do not treat perceiving as a form of thinking will include perceiving among the phenomena to be discussed under the heading 'mind'. They will populate the mind with sensory phenomena, not just intellectual ones:

> [O]ur senses, conversant about particular sensible objects, do convey into the mind several distinct perceptions, according to those various ways wherein those objects do affect them. (John Locke, *An Essay concerning Human Understanding* [1690], II 1, 3)

> All the perceptions of the human mind resolve themselves into two distinct kinds ... Those perceptions, which enter with most force and violence, we may name impressions; and under this name I comprehend all our sensations, passions and emotions, as they make their first appearance in the soul. (David Hume, *An Enquiry concerning Human Understanding* [1748, I 1.1)

But my task on this occasion is to look backwards from Descartes, not forwards. Back some 900 years from Augustine's distaste for the newly coined word 'mentalis', 1600 from Aquinas. The words that will chiefly concern us from now on are ancient Greek: the noun *nous* and the corresponding verb *noein*. And the philosopher whose dealings with them I shall be discussing is Aristotle. I shall suggest that his vocabulary is even more innovative than Descartes, but in the opposite direction. When compared with earlier philosophy, Descartes broadened the scope of mind. When compared with earlier philosophy, Aristotle greatly narrowed the scope of *nous, noein*.[13]

2.

My project, then, is to look at the way these two terms are used and analyzed in Aristotle without making the standard assumption that he and we are looking at the same object, viz. the workings of the mind, in such a way that we can compare what he says with the object about which he says it, and then ask which element in that object it is that he calls *nous, noein* and whether he characterizes it accurately, interestingly, or plausibly. If we do this, we are likely to suppose, as many scholars do suppose, that his topic is what we call thinking—and then we will be quite baffled to make sense of his remarks.

D.W. Hamlyn in his well-known Clarendon Aristotle Series commentary on the *De Anima* (1968, 103) is baffled. He complains of a constant tendency in Aristotle to run together thinking and knowing. Now when I say that Aristotle is not talking about what we call thinking, I do not mean that

he is talking about something quite else instead,
some other element of this neutral object, and that
we should change the translation to 'intuition', say,
or 'knowledge'. He is talking about some of the
things we use the notion of thinking to talk about,
but our 'thinking' and his *nous* are part and parcel
of a distinctive approach to man and nature. Our
conceptualization and his may be comparable as
wholes, but they are certainly not comparable in
separate pieces. Hence the extreme difficulty of
translating Aristotle's longest and most sustained
discussion of *nous*, *noein*: *De Anima* III 4-8.

These points may be illustrated by one of the
most widely consulted translations of the *De
Anima*, that of J.A. Smith in the renowned *Oxford
Translation of Aristotle*, first published in 1931
and recently revised by Jonathan Barnes for *The
Complete Works of Aristotle: The Revised Oxford
Translation* (1984). The faults of this translation
when it comes to *DA* III 4-8 are certainly not
due to inadequate familiarity with ancient Greek.
Smith, who taught at Balliol College, Oxford,
until in 1910 he was elected Waynflete Professor of
Metaphysics and Morals, was a man 'deeply versed
in philology ... [who] acquired with extraordinary
facility at least a reading knowledge of many languages. He had a very acute feeling for the precise
meaning, and the development of the meaning, of
words.'[14] Barnes' lively and many-sided contribu-

tions to our understanding of ancient philosophy and logic rank him as Smith's most distinguished successor in the great tradition of Balliol tutors. Let us then open *De Anima* III 4 and consider the following sentence at 430a 2-3: αὐτὸς [*sc. ὁ νοῦς*] δὲ νοητός ἐστιν ὥσπερ τὰ νοητά.

In *The Revised Oxford Translation* this reads, 'Thought is itself thinkable in exactly the same way as its objects are'. On first encounter I took this to be Smith's wording; I supposed that his keen admiration of the Idealist philosophy of Croce and Gentile might have made him more tolerant of such a sentence than some others would be. In fact, it is Barnes' revision. Smith originally wrote, 'Mind is itself thinkable in exactly the same way as its objects are'. Barnes preferred to mirror the verbal connection between the noun *nous* and the adjective *noētos*. Smith opted for a more substance-like English designation of the item we are to focus on. The trouble is that *both* translators obliterate a crucial difference which Aristotle emphasises quite early in the treatise:

> Lastly, certain living beings—a small minority—possess calculation and thought (λογισμὸν καὶ διάνοιαν), for (among mortal beings) those which possess calculation have all the other powers above mentioned, while the converse does not hold—indeed some live by imagination (φαντασία) alone, while others have not even imagination. *Theōrētikos*

nous presents a different problem (περὶ δὲ τοῦ
θεωρητικοῦ <u>νοῦ</u> ἕτερος λόγος). (*DA* I 3, 415a
7-12; tr. Smith)[15]

The crucial difference is that expressed by two
distinct Greek words, *dianoia* and *nous*. Both Smith
and Barnes use 'thought' for *dianoia*—rightly so,
for the word denotes a power possessed and exer-
cised by all humans. Together with *logismos* (cal-
culation, or better: reasoning) it constitutes the
specific difference of human beings. Both here and
elsewhere Aristotle marks off the species human
within the genus animal by humans' possession of
logismos and *dianoia*,[16] which I propose to render
'reasoning and thought'. The human species con-
sists of reasoning, thinking animals.

The second Greek word is *nous*—here qualified
as *theōrētikos nous*. Smith's rendering of the phrase
was 'the mind that knows with immediate intuition'. Barnes crossed that out and wrote 'reflective
thought' instead, which to me sounds considerably
less strenuous. Here again Smith wins the prize,
because we will soon see that *nous* is a rare achievement, not something to be had by musing, pipe
in hand, by the fireside. Either way, *theōrētikos*
normally contrasts with *praktikos* as 'theoretical'
to 'practical', so I shall speak simply of 'theoretical
nous'.[17] The question now becomes why Aristotle
should say that this *nous* is 'a different problem'

(Smith) or, as I would put it, another subject, for another discussion.

This is not the first time the *De Anima* has made such a claim. The passage just quoted chimes with three earlier statements which insist that *nous* is special, even divine, and is not to be treated on a par with ordinary thinking (*dianoeisthai*).[18] Aristotle has remarkably little to say about ordinary thought and thinking, either in this or any other of his works, but *nous* gets three whole chapters to itself here and an important discussion at the end of the *Posterior Analytics*, not to mention regular asides in *De Anima* Book I plus sustained attention in the theological context of *Metaphysics* Λ 7 and 9. I conclude that, while Aristotle takes thinking more or less for granted, *nous* is a distinct topic—and one on which he means to shine.

I shall translate *nous* as 'intellect', the verb *noein* as 'understand', hoping that by the end of this lecture these versions will strike you as appropriate, perhaps even compelling.

3.

The place to start is *De Anima* III 4 and the triple scheme, as I like to call it, of first and second potentiality, first and second actuality. Originally invoked in *De Anima* II 1 as the key to explaining soul or life itself, then elaborated, in II 5's complicated account of perception, it returns, in III 4 to explain *nous*:-

	Pot. 1	Pot. 2 / Act. 1	Act. 2
Model:	Man a knower by nature	Having learned to read & write	Using one's literacy read & write
for (i):		Power of → perception	Perceiving
and (ii):	Power of → thought & reasoning	Achieved intellectual power	Actual exercise of intellectual power

The power of perception has already reached second potentiality = first actuality when an animal emerges from womb, egg or slime (*DA* II 5, 417a 16-18). All it has to do to start actually gaining information about the world is open its eyes to see or explore with its means of touch. The intellectual powers accessible to humans come more slowly, through time and effort. All we are born with is the *capacity* to think and reason, which we must train and use if we are to arrive at theoretical understanding of the world.[19]

Now let me introduce the identity thesis. According to Aristotle, when an animal opens its eyes and sees red, what happens is that the eyes in some sense take on that colour or, as he also puts it, they become red in a way (*DA* III 8, 431b 20-432a 3). Seeing red is becoming red. Not surprisingly, it is much debated what exactly this thesis means. Aristotle makes a parallel claim about the intellect:

Νῦν δὲ περὶ ψυχῆς τὰ λεχθέντα συγκεφαλαιώσαντες εἴπωμεν πάλιν ὅτι ἡ ψυχὴ τὰ ὄντα πώς ἐστιν· πάντα γὰρ ἢ αἰσθητὰ τὰ ὄντα ἢ νοητά, ἔστι δ᾽ ἡ ἐπιστήμη μὲν τὰ ἐπιστητά πως, ἡ δ᾽ αἴσθησις τὰ αἰσθητά.

And now let us sum up what has been said concerning the soul by repeating that in a manner the soul is all the things that are. For the things that are are all either objects of perception or objects of intellect,[20] and knowledge is in a way the things that are knowable, perception in a way the things that are perceptible. (*DA* III 8, 431b 20-23)[21]

This is not the occasion for me to revisit long-standing controversies about Aristotle's theory of perception.[22] I merely pause to note this text's emphasis on the parallelism between perception and intellectual knowledge. Each is said to become their object in some way. It is widely agreed in the scholarly literature that no underlying material processes or conditions are involved when the intellect becomes its object by taking on an intelligible form. Not everyone agrees with me

that no underlying material *processes* are involved
when perception becomes its object by taking
on a perceptible form, only a standing material
state of receptivity in the sense organ (transparent
eye-jelly in the eye, still air in the ear, etc.). I suggest that those who insist on underlying material
processes for perception, but not for intellectual
understanding, owe us an explanation of why
Aristotle should tolerate such a significant lack
of parallelism between the two types of cognition
whose parallelism he trumpets both in the passage
just quoted and elsewhere (III 4, 429a 13-18).

That said, I turn to the question of where in
the triple scheme to locate the intellectual identity which parallels the identity of sense with its
object. In the case of perception the answer is clear:
at the transition from first actuality (= second
potentiality) to second actuality, marked → in
the diagram. For example, when you wake up in
the morning and open your eyes to see the white
colour of your pillow. When you go to sleep you
do not lose the power of sight, which throughout
the night remains at second potentiality = first
actuality.

For the intellect many scholars give the parallel
answer: the identity is achieved at the transition
between first and second actuality.[23] Here is the
proof text which shows unambiguously that that is
wrong:

ὅταν δ᾿ οὕτως ἕκαστα γένηται [*sc.* ὁ νοῦς] ὡς ὁ
ἐπιστήμων λέγεται ὁ κατ᾿ ἐνέργειαν (<u>τοῦτο δὲ</u>
<u>συμβαίνει, ὅταν δύνηται ἐνεργεῖν δι᾿ αὑτοῦ</u>), ἔστι
μὲν καὶ τότε δυνάμει πως, οὐ μὴν ὁμοίως καὶ πρὶν
μαθεῖν ἢ εὑρεῖν.

When the intellect becomes each thing in the way
in which an actual knower does[24] (*which happens
as soon as the knower can exercise their power of their
own accord*), even then it is still in one sense just a
capacity: not, however, a capacity in the same sense
as before it learned or discovered. (III 4, 429b 5-9;
tr. after Hicks and Hamlyn, emphasis mine)

As marked by the second → in the diagram, the
identity of intellect with its object holds already
at second potentiality = first actuality, *before* the
knower switches to the second actuality of exercis-
ing that intellectual power of their own accord.

I do not mean that the identity ceases to hold
when second actuality is achieved. On the contrary,
the form already acquired is then actively guid-
ing the knower's thought.[25] The difference is that
sensible objects are particular and external to the
perceiving subject, so that it is not up to us what
sensible forms impinge on our senses, whereas
scientific knowledge (*epistēmē*) is of universals
and these, once learned, are said to reside 'in a
way' in the soul itself. In consequence, we can
activate our knowledge of them when we please
(II 5, 418a 19-26). Just this is the stage indicated

by the italicized clause 'as soon as the knower can exercise their power of their own accord'.

The final preliminary is to consider what Aristotle means when he glosses first actuality knowledge of an intelligible form as the knower's having acquired, taken on, or become that form. In Aristotle, as in Plato, to know an intelligible form is to have mastered and internalized a definition. Not any old definition of something, but the scientifically correct definition of its essence. Now an Aristotelian essence is rather more than a common feature, more even than a set of necessary and sufficient conditions for being a so-and-so. It is a first principle of explanatory demonstration. To find the essence of a kind is to find the cause or explanation of the various properties that necessarily belong to members of the kind in virtue of their being that kind of thing. In Aristotle's language, the explananda are the *per se* attributes (*ta kath' hauta sumbebēkota*), the essence the explanans. It is this powerful explanatory principle that is said to be taken on or acquired by the knower at the stage of second potentiality = first actuality knowledge.

Thus the form of lion exists, as one might put it, in two modes. In the lion it is first and foremost the essence which explains the various features that typify a lion and its life. In Aristotle's technical talk these explananda are the *per se* features of lion life, the features that belong to lions *qua* lions, i.e. features that all lions possess because they are lions. A modern analogue to the essence that comprehensively explains all such features might be a lion's genetic code. Secondly, however, the form or essence of lion exists also in the intellect of a zoologist who has internalized a secure understanding of that essence and its power to explain the traits that belong to all lions because they are lions leading a lion's life. This would match a zoologist's drawing up the map of a lion's genetic code.

Such a cause will take some finding. But Aristotle offers some heuristic advice:

ἔοικε δ᾽ οὐ μόνον τὸ τί ἐστι γνῶναι χρήσιμον εἶναι πρὸς τὸ θεωρῆσαι τὰς αἰτίας τῶν συμβεβηκότων ταῖς οὐσίαις, ὥσπερ ἐν τοῖς μαθήμασιν οἷον τί τὸ εὐθὺ καὶ τί τὸ καμπύλον ἢ τί γραμμὴ καὶ ἐπίπεδον πρὸς τὸ κατιδεῖν πόσαις ὀρθαῖς αἱ τοῦ τριγώνου γωνίαι ἴσαι, ἀλλὰ καὶ ἀνάπαλιν τὰ συμβεβηκότα συμβάλλεται μέγα μέρος πρὸς τὸ εἰδέναι τὸ τί ἐστιν· ἐπειδὰν γὰρ ἔχωμεν ἀποδιδόναι κατὰ τὴν φαντασίαν περὶ τῶν συμβεβηκότων, ἢ πάντων ἢ τῶν πλείστων, τότε καὶ περὶ τῆς οὐσίας ἕξομεν λέγειν κάλλιστα· πάσης γὰρ ἀποδείξεως ἀρχὴ τὸ τί ἐστιν, ὥστε καθ᾽ ὅσους τῶν ὁρισμῶν μὴ συμβαίνει τὰ συμβεβηκότα γνωρίζειν, ἀλλὰ μηδ᾽ εἰκάσαι περὶ αὐτῶν εὐμαρές, δῆλον ὅτι διαλεκτικῶς εἴρηνται καὶ κενῶς ἅπαντες.

It seems that not only is the knowledge of a thing's essential nature useful for discovering the causes of its attributes (as in mathematics ascertaining what straight and curved are, or line and surface, is useful for seeing how many right angles the angles of a triangle are equal to), but also, conversely, the attributes contribute greatly to the knowledge of what a thing is. For it is when we are able to give an account of all, or at any rate most, of the attributes *as they appear to us* that we shall best be able to speak about the essence too. For the starting point of every demonstration is what a thing is, hence definitions which lead to no information about attributes, or do not even help us conjecture about them, are clearly all just dialectical and empty. (*DA* I 1, 402b 16-403a 2; tr. after Hicks and Hamlyn)

The idea is that you should familiarize yourself with the full range of the attributes to be explained, because it is when you can give a provisional account[26] of all or most of these that you will be best placed to determine the essence which is the starting point of explanatory demonstration. How do lions, for example, reproduce, digest their food, cope with their habitat? How well do they perceive, or track their prey? What is their life cycle? And so on. A carefully detailed knowledge of what needs to be explained is the best preparation for an attempt to formulate an adequate explanation.

It appears, then, that we will not finally be in a position to fix the essence of lion until we have a pretty thorough preliminary knowledge of the species. Then, and then only, can we identify and define the substantial form which makes a lion what it is and gives unity to the various phenomena we have been studying. For the form, according to Aristotle, just is the essence which explains the remaining necessary characteristics that belong to any lion by virtue of its being that kind of thing. And among these necessary characteristics we must of course include the matter which is correlative to lion form. The physical world is not pre-stocked with lion matter as it is with copper and iron; it takes an actual pre-existing lion to take in the relevant foodstuffs from which lion matter is then made, and the principle which explains that manufacturing process is, once again, the soul, form or essence of lion (*DA* II 4).

In sum, an Aristotelian form is not to be grasped on its own, as a solitary item of knowledge, but only as part and pinnacle of a whole explanatory system. Well may one wonder whether such a grasp is within ordinary human reach. Aristotle repeatedly reserves the name *nous, noein* for this achievement. When he says, for example, that *nous* is the disposition that grasps the first principles of a deductive science (*APo.* II 19, 100 b 5-17; *EN* VI 6; cf. *Met.* A 2, 982a 19-b 10), he clearly means

grasping them *as* the starting points of elaborate
explanatory deductions. A single sentence, this
hints, could never be an adequate expression of
achieved *nous*.

4.

Here I pause to gather some of the things Aristotle
says about his God in Books I and II of the *De
Anima*.

   (1) In the very first chapter he raises the
question whether all attributes (*pathē*) of soul are
shared (perhaps better: shared in) by the body it
animates, or are there some that belong exclusively
(*idia*) to soul? In most cases, he says, soul's being
affected or acting does seem to involve the body as
well; this is true of being angry or confident, desiring and, in general, perceiving.[27] The most plausible exception would seem to be *noein*—unless
this depends on a body either because it is itself
some kind of appearance (*phantasia*) or because
it cannot function without appearance (403a 3-
10).[28] The conclusion is that if, and only if, there is
some function or affection of soul which is exclu-
sive to it, i.e. which does not involve body as well
as soul, then it would be possible for soul to exist
separately, on its own (403a 10-16: *endechoit' an
autēn chērizesthai*). Suppose *noein* is such a function or affection of soul. Then there could be a

kind of soul which had intellect but no body, just as at the other end of the *scala naturae* there can be and is a kind of soul, the nutritive-reproductive soul of plants, which *dunatai chōrizesthai tēs haphēs kai pasēs aisthēseōs*: a kind of soul which can and does exist without any of the cognitive powers that distinguish animals (II 2, 413a 20-b 10).

I emphasise the parallel with plant souls lest anyone take the passage to be scouting the idea that a human individual's intellect might survive their death to continue functioning on its own. Aristotle is obviously not saying that an animal's nutritive-reproductive powers could be separated out for installation in a plant body. Nor then is he contemplating a bodyless immortality for the individual intellect of Socrates. He is wondering about an intellect which of its own nature functions quite independently of bodies and their powers. This is our first intimation of the divine intellect of *De Anima* III 5 and *Metaphysics* Λ.

(2) The second intimation comes later in Book I from a passage which *inter alia* confirms that *nous/noein* is not at all the same thing as *dianoia/ dianoeisthai*. Translators constantly ignore this non-identity, rendering both nouns and both verbs as 'thought' and 'thinking'.[29] The result is a chaos and confusion that I will document in footnotes. For those without Greek, let me just nominate the

passage as, currently, the worst translated passage
in ancient philosophy:-

τὸ δὴ λέγειν ὀργίζεσθαι τὴν ψυχὴν ὅμοιον κἂν εἴ
τις λέγοι τὴν ψυχὴν ὑφαίνειν ἢ οἰκοδομεῖν· βέλτιον
γὰρ ἴσως μὴ λέγειν τὴν ψυχὴν ἐλεεῖν ἢ μανθάνειν
ἢ διανοεῖσθαι, ἀλλὰ τὸν ἄνθρωπον τῇ ψυχῇ·
τοῦτο δὲ μὴ ὡς ἐν ἐκείνῃ τῆς κινήσεως οὔσης,
ἀλλ' ὁτὲ μὲν μέχρι ἐκείνης, ὁτὲ δ' ἀπ' ἐκείνης,
οἷον ἡ μὲν αἴσθησις ἀπὸ τωνδί, ἡ δ' ἀνάμνησις
ἀπ' ἐκείνης ἐπὶ τὰς ἐν τοῖς αἰσθητηρίοις κινήσεις
ἢ μόνας.

ὁ δὲ νοῦς ἔοικεν ἐγγίνεσθαι οὐσία τις οὖσα, καὶ οὐ
φθείρεσθαι.[30] μάλιστα γὰρ ἐφθείρετ' ἂν ὑπὸ τῆς
ἐν τῷ γήρᾳ ἀμαυρώσεως, νῦν δ' ὥσπερ ἐπὶ τῶν
αἰσθητηρίων συμβαίνει· εἰ γὰρ λάβοι ὁ πρεσβύτης
ὄμμα τοιοδί, βλέποι ἂν ὥσπερ καὶ ὁ νέος. ὥστε
τὸ γῆρας οὐ τῷ τὴν ψυχήν τι πεπονθέναι, ἀλλ'
ἐν ᾧ, καθάπερ ἐν μέθαις καὶ νόσοις. καὶ τὸ
νοεῖν δὴ καὶ τὸ θεωρεῖν μαραίνεται ἄλλου τινὸς
ἔσω φθειρομένου, αὐτὸ δὲ ἀπαθές ἐστιν. τὸ δὲ
διανοεῖσθαι καὶ φιλεῖν ἢ μισεῖν οὐκ ἔστιν ἐκείνου
πάθη, ἀλλὰ τουδὶ τοῦ ἔχοντος ἐκεῖνο, ᾗ ἐκεῖνο
ἔχει. διὸ καὶ τούτου φθειρομένου οὔτε μνημονεύει
οὔτε φιλεῖ· οὐ γὰρ ἐκείνου ἦν, ἀλλὰ τοῦ κοινοῦ,
ὃ ἀπόλωλεν· ὁ δὲ νοῦς ἴσως θειότερόν τι καὶ
ἀπαθές ἐστιν.

To say that the soul is angry is like saying that the
soul weaves or builds. I mean: it is surely better not
to say that the soul pities, *learns or thinks*, but that
the human being does this with their soul, and this

not because the movement takes place in the soul, but because sometimes it reaches to the soul and at other times comes from it; e.g. perception starts from these things around us, while recollection starts from the soul and reaches to movements or remnants in the sense-organs.

It would seem that *intellect*, on the other hand, comes to reside in us as a kind of substance, and one not subject to destruction.[31] If anything could destroy it, it would be the feebleness of old age. As things are, what happens is doubtless just like what happens to the sense-organs. If an aged man could procure an eye of the right sort, he would see just as well as a youngster. Hence old age is not due to the soul's being affected in a certain way—what is affected is that [*sc.* the body] in which the soul resides, as is the case with drunkenness and disease. In like manner, then, understanding and contemplation[32] decline because something else within is destroyed, while in itself it is unaffected.[33] But thinking (διανοεῖσθαι)[34] and loving or hating are not affections of *that* [*sc.* the intellect], but of *this* thing [*sc.* the human being] which possesses that, to the extent that it does so possess it. Hence also, when *this* [the human] perishes there is neither remembering nor loving. For these never did belong to *that* [the intellect],[35] but to the thing which shared in it [the human] and which has now perished. The *intellect*, on the other hand, is doubtless a thing more divine and one that cannot be affected. (I 4, 408b 11-29)

This text not only confirms my previous insistence on distinguishing between *nous* and ordinary thinking (*dianoia*). It implies (a) that *nous*, unlike ordinary thought, is divine and immortal, (b) that it can come to reside *in* a human being as itself an extra kind of substance, distinct from the mortal substance it resides in, and (c) that it remains completely unaffected by the death of its temporary human vehicle. This text also says, twice and with some emphasis, that *dianoia*, like love and hate, does not belong to *nous*.

(3) The issue of separate existence returns in II 2, 413b 24-32:

> About intellect and the contemplative[36] faculty (περὶ δὲ τοῦ νοῦ καὶ τῆς θεωρητικῆς δυνάμεως) nothing is clear as yet. But it looks to be a generically different kind of soul, and this alone can be separate(d), as the eternal is separate(d) from the perishable.[37] What is clear from these considerations is that the remaining parts of the soul are *not* separate, despite what some say. In account they are different, to be sure, given that perceiving is different from believing/ judging, and similarly with the other faculties mentioned.

Aristotle does not yet definitely affirm the conclusion he is attracted to, but here again he makes it perfectly clear that the faculty of *thinking, believing, judging* (413b 13: *to dianoētikon*; b 30: *to doxastikon*) is *not* what he inclined to classify as a generically different, because eternal and divine, kind of soul. That honour is reserved for whatever it is that he calls *nous, to noētikon, to noein.*

5.

Let these points take us back to *De Anima* III 4 to see how smoothly it leads on to *De Anima* III 5 and *Metaphysics* Λ:

> About the part of the soul by which the soul knows and has sound judgement (ᾧ γινώσκει τε ἡ ψυχὴ καὶ φρονεῖ)[38]—regardless of whether it is separate, or not separate in magnitude but only in account—we must inquire what its differentia is and how intellectual understanding comes about (καὶ πῶς ποτὲ γίνεται τὸ νοεῖν).

> Now if intellectual understanding (τὸ νοεῖν)[39] is akin to perceiving, it will be a case either of being affected by the intelligible object (πάσχειν τι ἂν εἴη ὑπὸ τοῦ νοητοῦ), or something similar to that. It must then, while itself impassive (ἀπαθές), be receptive to the form and potentially like it without being it, and *as the faculty of perception is to perceptible things, so must nous be to intelligible objects* (οὕτως τὸν νοῦν πρὸς τὰ νοητά). It is necessary, therefore, since it understands everything (ἐπεὶ πάντα νοεῖ),[40] that it be unmixed, as Anaxagoras says, in order that it may master its objects, that is, know (γνωρίζῃ) them (for the intrusion of anything foreign interferes with it). As a result

*it has no nature of its own other than its potential to
become this or that.* Accordingly, the so-called *nous*
of the soul- *by 'nous' I mean that by which the soul
thinks and judges* (διανοεῖται καὶ ὑπολαμβάνει)
- is in actuality none of the things that are before
it understands them (πρὶν νοεῖν). That is why
it is reasonable for it not to be mixed with the
body; this would result in its being of some qual-
ity, either cold or hot, and it would have an organ
as the perceptive faculty does. But as it is, it is not
anything. And people do well to say that the soul
is the place of forms, *except that it is not the whole
of soul that is this, only the noetic soul,* nor is it the
forms in actuality, only in potentiality. And that the
impassivity of the perceptive is different from that
of the noetic faculties is clear from the sense-organs
and perception. Perception is incapacitated by an
excessive object such a very loud sound, and one
cannot see an excessively bright colour or endure
an excessively strong smell. But when the intellect
has understood an extremely intelligible item, it
understands lesser things better, not worse. For
*the perceptual faculty cannot function apart from
the body, but the intellect is separate* (τὸ μὲν γὰρ
αἰσθητικὸν οὐκ ἄνευ σώματος, ὁ δὲ χωριστός).
And when the intellect becomes each thing in the
way in which an actual knower does (*which happens
as soon as the knower can exercise their power of their
own accord*) ... (III 4, 429a 10-b 7)

I have quoted enough of this text to show where
it joins on to my earlier quotation at p. 23, from

which I concluded that the identity between intellect and intelligibles takes place at first actuality = second potentiality. It follows that the stage prior to the achievement of identity is first potentiality. It is therefore *first* potentiality *nous* which is described at 429a 23 as 'that by which the soul thinks and judges'.

This is a novelty, signalled by the word λέγω ('I mean' = 'I here mean'). To appreciate its significance, turn the sentence around: that by which the soul thinks and judges is first potentiality *nous*. Which is to say that the human capacity for thinking and judging, a capacity we are born with alongside the capacity to reason—the two capacities together comprising our differentia as a biological species—gives us the potential to grasp the intelligible forms which explain the world as it is objectively speaking. For example, just in virtue of our being what it is to be a human being we all have a potential to attain a complete and accurate, totally objective understanding of lion life. The capacity for ordinary thinking (*dianoia*) can after all be titled *nous*—and was so titled already at II 3, 414b 18: *to dianoētikon te kai nous*—but only in the sense of first potentiality.

Lots of human lives never advance to second potentiality *nous* about anything. They are not on that account (to be) judged failures, for not all of us are called to intellectual achievement on a par with mastering the genetic code of lions. Nonetheless, Aristotle's claim is that mere membership of the human species gives us, in some importantly real sense, the potential to do so.[41]

This is the claim which Alfred Russell Wallace thought inexplicable in evolutionary terms. With that, of course, Aristotle would happily agree, on principle and not only because of the crude simplicities of the evolutionary theories he was acquainted with. The principle is an exceedingly strong version of the principle of the priority of the actual, meaning temporal priority, not just priority in the order of understanding. Any instance of being potentially such-and-such is preceded by an instance of something else being actually such-and-such (*Met.* Θ 8, 1049b 10-50a 3). More simply, there is nothing new under the Sun—nor, of course, above the Sun, given the unchanging circulation of the stars in the Aristotelian universe.

Aristocles of Messana (2nd cent. AD), teacher of the great commentator Alexander of Aphrodisias, said that two things are driving (*kinounta*) Aristotle when he propounds the theory of the Agent Intellect in *De Anima* III 5: one is the analogy between nous and perception, the other the principle of the priority of actuality over potentiality.[42] I believe that these two things are indeed enough to enable us to read the chapter as an ancient Greek version of Wallace's conviction that appeal to God is necessary to explain the fact that man's mind so far exceeds in capacity what is required for ordinary human life and the continuity of the species.

6.

Let us go back to the parallel Aristotle insistently draws between perception and intellectual knowledge. I said that, in the case of a lion, its first actuality (lion soul) is simultaneously a second potentiality both (i) for stalking proudly about the land and (ii) for being known and understood by the scientist who studies lions (a leontologist?). Analogously, the golden-brown colour of a lion is both (i) what makes it actually brown, and (ii) its potentiality for being seen (as brown). But we can make the correspondence neater still.

Aristotle holds, and at least in the case of colour, sound and smells we agree, that an enabling condition for the perception of sensible qualities is a medium through which they can be cognized.[43] For sight, the necessary medium is air or water in a state of actual transparency, which state of actual transparency Aristotle equates with light. Light in his physics does not travel (he berates Empedocles for his idiocy in thinking it does): it is a *state* of air or water, the state in which it is actually transparent so that things can be seen through it. More formally, light is the actuality of the transparent qua transparent.[44] Now a central thesis of *De Anima* III 5 is the following: as light is a condition for the stage which precedes the taking on of visible form, i.e. prior to sight's becoming colour(ed), so there is something *like* light (430a 15) which is a condition prior to the identity of knower and known. Like light, this too is a state (*hexis tis*), not a movement of some kind. And it is said to *make* everything in a way that parallels the way light makes colours actually visible. In context this must mean that it makes things actually know*able*.

We are now ready for the notoriously brief and crabby text of *De Anima* III 5. By way of preface, let me suggest a reason for its brevity. The *De Anima* is a treatise in physics or second philosophy, firmly embedded by a network of cross-references within the series that runs from *Physics* to the biological works.[45] But III 5, as I propose to interpret it, is first philosophy, theology, metaphysics. For it is wholly focussed on God, the Divine Intellect. Now elsewhere Aristotle shows himself concerned lest physics, by encroaching on topics that are the proper concern of first philosophy, leave no scope for the supreme science to operate independently (*PA* I 1, 641a 32-b 12; *Met.* VI 1). That worry would be reason enough to keep III 5's excursion into theology as brief as possible.

This does not excuse the crabby style, which continues until III 9 embarks on a whole new section devoted to animal movement. The crabbiness ensures that translation of III 5 is entwined with interpretation at every step. The following translation-cum-interpretation of the chapter is offered as a plausible climax to the various interpretative choices embedded in the translations presented so far:

Since, as[46] in the whole of nature there is something which serves as matter to each kind[47] (*viz.* that which is potentially all the members of the kind), and something else which serves as cause and producer to the kind, by producing all its members, the two being related to one another as art to its material—since that is so, of necessity these same distinctions must obtain also in the sphere of soul.[48] Thus there is one kind of intellect that exists by becoming all things, and another that exists by making all things—making them in the way a dispositional state (ἕξις) such as light makes things; for in a way light does in fact make potential colours actual colours. And this latter intellect is separate, and nothing can affect it, and it mixes with nothing else—all because its very being is actuality (τῇ οὐσίᾳ ὢν ἐνέργεια).[49] For[50] always that which acts is of higher worth[51] than that which is acted upon, the originative principle than the matter. Now actual knowledge (ἡ κατ' ἐνέργειαν ἐπιστήμη) is identical with the thing known. Potential knowledge is prior in time in any single individual, but it is not prior in time quite generally,[52] because the intellect under discussion[53] is not a thing that

exercises its understanding at some times while at
other times it does not. And being separated [*sc.*
from everything else],[54] it is what it is essentially
and nothing else. And this alone is immortal and
eternal. Yet we do not remember because[55] this is
impassive (ἀπαθές), whereas the passive intellect
(ὁ παθητικὸς νοῦς) is perishable. And without this
nothing understands (νοεῖ).[56]

The punch line, as I see it, comes at the very
end.

'This' recurs in each of the last three sentences,
in the second of which it contrasts with the 'we'
implicit in the first person plural present tense form
of the Greek verb 'to remember'. So 'this' is not 'we'
and none of us is 'this'. 'This' alone is immortal,
so 'we' are not. Nor is 'the passive intellect', intro-
duced earlier as the kind of intellect which exists
by 'becoming', i.e. by coming to understand, all
things. But if and when the passive intellect does
come to understand a thing or two, it cannot—the
final sentence announces—do so without 'this'.
Our mortal intellect needs an immortal intellect
to achieve its goal of understanding.

How does the immortal intellect help us? How
does it make things intelligible to our mortal
minds? Simply by existing, I would suggest, by
being what it is: an eternal intellect constituted,
like any other intellect, as a system of concepts.
The difference is that the divine intellect is a system

(better, perhaps, *the* system) of absolutely correct concepts. As such, the deity does not need to act on us from up high, but merely to illuminate the intelligible forms, somewhat in the way light, simply in virtue of being what it is, illuminates colours and makes them actually visible to us.

Here I should emphasize that light, in Aristotle's view, is itself a *state* of a medium such as air or water. Light neither travels nor, unless it is dazzlingly bright, does it affect our eyes.[57] It merely enables colours to affect our sight. Just so, we must suppose, Aristotle's divine intellect does nothing but be what it is. Like light, it is a state, not a process. As light is a state of a material medium which makes the visible forms (colours) actually visible to sight, so the divine intellect is cast as a non-material medium through which the intelligible forms become apparent to the human intellect. Put the other way round, it enables the knower to 'see through' to the forms, to understand them as they really are. The comparison which comes to mind is that limiting case of perspective which certain philosophers have called the absolute viewpoint or the point of view of the universe. To take up that 'viewpoint' is to get yourself in a position to see how things really and objectively are.

To those who have read Plato's *Republic* all this should sound incredibly familiar. As the light of the Sun makes sensible things visible and gives us the ability to see them, so the Good makes the intelligible Forms knowable and gives our intellect (our *nous*, the eye of the soul) the ability to know them. If Aristotle substitutes the first principle and best thing in his universe for the first principle and best thing in Plato's universe and leaves the analogy otherwise untouched, the result will be the theory that Alexander, the best and most purely Aristotelian of the ancient commentators, found in *De Anima* III 5; the theory that Brentano dismissed as 'prattle without all sense and reason'.[58] The Active Intellect is God.[59]

At this point it is appropriate to recall that in the Aristotelian universe all nature imitates the deity. It is as final cause that God is the Prime Mover of everything, starting with the most basic material elements (earth, air, fire and water) whose ceaseless interchange is their way of achieving constancy in imitation of the eternal first cause (GC II 10, 336b 25-337a 15; *Met.* Θ8, 1050b 28-30). Next come the constant reproductive cycles of living things, plants as well as animals (*DA* II 4, 415a 26-b 7; *GA* II 1, 731b 24-732a 11). Finally, it is because God's life of contemplation is the best mode of existence in the universe, and the most pleasant, that for us humans too cognitive activity is the most pleasant: not just noetic contemplation, but also states that God does not share such as waking and perceiving, hopes and memories (*Met.* Λ7,

1072b 13-24). What is special about the exercise of *nous*, the highest form of cognition that humans can attain, is that it is no longer a more or less distant imitation of the divine life. It is a limited span of the very same activity as God enjoys for all time.

This is the key to Aristotle's recommendation of the contemplative life in *Nicomachean Ethics* X 7, 1177b 26-34. We should not to follow 'those who advise us, being men, to think of human things, and, being mortal, of mortal things'. Instead, we should, 'make ourselves immortal so far as we can' (ἐφ' ὅσον ἐνδέχεται ἀθανατίζειν). To make ourselves immortal, to enjoy for a while the same understanding as God has, what is this but the other side of the *De Anima*'s idea (above p. 31) that intellect 'comes to reside in us as a kind of substance, and one not subject to destruction'? Or to put it another way,

If, then, God is always in that good state in which we sometimes are, this compels our wonder; and if in a better, this compels it yet more. And God *is* in a better state. (*Met.* Λ7, 1072b24-6; tr. Ross) [60]

NOTES

1 I use the neuter because ancient Greek θεός, like
ἄνθρωπος, is grammatically both masculine and
feminine, taking both the masculine and feminine
articles; moreover, there are occasions when ὁ θεός/
ἄνθρωπος refers to a female.

2 Augustine, *De genesi ad litteram* 12, 7: 'Tria genera
visionum ... corporale, spirituale, ... tertium vero
intellectuale ab intellectu, quia mentale a mente ipsa
vocabuli novitate nimis absurdum est ut dicamus'.

3 Aquinas, *ST* 1a2ae, *q.* 56, 3 *a.* 3: '*Sed contra* est quod
mens maxime dicitur intellectus. Subjectum autem
virtutis est mens, ut patet ex definitione virtutis supra
inducta. Ergo intellectus est subjectum virtutis.'

4 *ST* 1a2ae, *q.* 55, *a.* 4, citing Augustine, *De Trini-
tate* XII 3: 'Ubi primo occurrit aliquid quod non
sit nobis pecoribusque commune, illud ad mentem
pertinet'.

5 'De natura mentis humanae: quòd ipsa sit notior
quàm corpus'; French version: 'De la nature de
l'ésprit humain: et qu'il est plus aisé à connaître que
le corps'.

6 'Sum igitur praecise tantum res cogitans, id est,
mens, *sive animus*, sive intellectus, sive ratio', where
(as also n. 9 below) italics signal words not rendered
into the French version: 'je ne suis donc précisément
parlant qu'une chose qui pense, c'est à dire un Esprit,
un Entendement, ou une raison'.

7   Descartes' learned readers would know that the
     verb had a much wider range then than it does now.
     In particular, Cicero used it to Latinize the Stoics'
     καταλήψις, the unchallengeable cognitive grasp on
     which their epistemology was grounded.

8   '... corpora, non proprie a sensibus, vel ab imagi-
     nandi facultate, sed a solo intellectu percipi, nec ex
     eo percipi quòd tangantur aut videantur, sed tantùm
     ex eo quòd intelligantur ...'; French version: '... à
     proprement parler nous ne concevons les corps que
     par la faculté d'entendre qui est en nous, et non point
     par l'imagination ni par les sens, et que nous ne les
     connaissons pas de ce que nous les voyons, ou que
     nous les touchons, mais seulement de ce que nous
     les concevons par la pensée ...'

9   'Idem denique ego sum qui sentio, sive qui res cor-
     poreas tanquam per sensus animadverto: videlicet
     jam lucem video, strepitum audio, calorem sentio.
     Falsa haec sunt, dormio enim. At certe videre videor,
     audire, calescere. *Hoc falsum esse non potest*; hoc est
     proprie quod in me sentire appellatur; atque hoc
     praecise sic sumptum nihil aliud est quàm cogitare';
     French version: 'Enfin je suis le même qui sens,
     c'est-à-dire qui reçois et connais les choses comme
     par les organes des sens: puisqu'en effet je vois la
     lumière, j'ois le bruit, je ressens la chaleur. Mais l'on
     me dira que ces apparences sont fausses, et que je
     dors. Qu'il soit ainsi, toutefois à tout le moins il est
     très certain qu'il me semble que je vois, que j'ois, et
     que je m'échauffe, et c'est proprement ce qui en moi
     s'appelle sentir; et cela pris ainsi précisément n'est
     rien autre chose que penser.'

10   'Sed quid igitur sum? Res cogitans. Quid est hoc?
     Nempe dubitans, intelligens, affirmans, negans,

volens, nolens, imaginans quoque, & sentiens';
French version: 'Mais qu'est-ce donc que je suis? Une
chose qui pense; qu'est-ce qu'une chose qui pense?
C'est-à-dire une chose qui doute, qui conçoit, qui
affirme, qui nie, qui veut, qui ne veut pas, qui imagine
aussi, et qui sent.'

11 'Ego sum res cogitans, id est dubitans, affirmans,
    negans, pauca intelligens, multa ignorans, volens,
    nolens, imaginans etiam & sentiens; ut enim ante
    animadverti, quamvis illa quae sentio vel imaginor
    extra me nihil sint, illos tamen cogitandi modos,
    quos sensus & imaginationes appello, quatenus
    cogitandi quidam modi tantùm sunt, in me esse
    sum certus'; French version: 'Je suis une chose qui
    pense, c'est-à-dire une chose qui doute, qui conçoit,
    qui affirme, qui nie, qui connaît peu de choses, qui
    en ignore beaucoup, *qui aime, qui hait*, qui veut, qui
    ne veut pas, qui imagine aussi, et qui sent. Car, ainsi
    que j'ai remarqué ci-devant, quoique les choses que
    je sens et que j'imagine ne soient peut-être rien di
    tout hors de moi, *et en elles-mêmes*, je suis néanmois
    assuré que ces façons de penser, que j'appelle senti-
    ments et imaginations, en tant seulement qu'elles
    sont des façons de penser, résident et se rencontrent
    certainement en moi' (italics signal words added in
    the French edition).

12 So Rodis-Lewis in her Introduction, xii.

13 Book I of *De Anima* complains at some length
    about the Preocratics' failure to distinguish *nous* from
    lesser forms of cognition: I 2, 404a 27-b 6; 405a 9-17.
    For relevant discussion, see Frede 1996b.

14 Ross (1949), 818-20. My own appreciation of
    Smith (in Burnyeat 2005) is due to his obscurely
    named 'On General Relative Clauses in Greek'

(1917), in which his linguistic ingenuity annihilates the sole evidence for the common assumption that Plato posited a Form for every general term.

15 I note in passing that φαντασία is another pitfall for translators: the standard rendering 'imagination' fits a mere eight lines (427b 17-24) of the lengthy discussion devoted to the topic in *DA* III 3. The *mot juste* for the noun corresponding to the verb φαίνεσθαι is 'appearance', the sense given to it by Plato at *Tht.* 152bc, *Soph.* 264ab.

16 *DA* II 3, 414b 18-19; cf. I 5, 410b 24; II 2, 413b 12-13; 29-31; 414a 12-13; 3, 414a 31-2; *Met.* I 1, 980b 27-8.

17 The contrast between theoretical and practical νοῦς is discussed in *EN* VI 11, which is far from encouraging the idea that practical wisdom is unreflective.

18 See *DA* I 4, 408b 3-29; 5, 410b 12-15; II 2, 413b 24-32.

19 In Burnyeat 2002 I offer a lengthy exposition of the triple scheme and its significance.

20 Smith here renders 'existing things are either sensible or thinkable', but continues 'and knowledge is in a way what is knowable'.

21 Translations not otherwise accredited are my own.

22 My most recent effort in this area is Burnyeat 2002. Caston (2004) gives a full and fair critical overview of the twists and turns of a long debate between myself, Richard Sorabji, and others.

23 So, for example, Lear chap. 4.3; Hadot 369 (citing II 1, 412a 10; 5, 417a 28, which merely distinguish second from first actuality without mention of

the identity), who, however, follows with a superb account of what the identity means in Plotinus.

24 Smith: 'Once the mind has become each set of its possible objects, as a man of science has, when this phrase is used of one who is actually a man of science'. Barnes: 'When thought has become each thing in the way in which a man who actually knows is said to do so'.

25 As spelled out, for the case of productive arts, in *Met.* Θ2.

26 ἀποδιδόναι κατὰ φαντασίαν: an account which renders how the attribute appears to a skilled scientific observer who does not yet command the explanation of why it is as it is. Smith and Barnes agree on 'for, when we are able to give an account conformable to experience of all or most of the properties of the substance ...'

27 Note that this last point says no more than that perceiving requires a body; it does not ascribe to that body some material process underlying the perception. If ὅλως at 403a 7 appears to subsume under perceiving the three items previously mentioned, *viz.* getting angry, being confident, and desiring, that fits III 7, 431a 8-14.

28 See n. 15 above for the translation of φαντασία.

29 Hicks *ad* 408b 18-29 does acknowledge 'the assumed distinction between διανοεῖσθαι and νοεῖν ', but only to add that it 'appears to me quite arbitrary, since either verb may stand for the act of thinking'! A good counterweight to this arrogance is Frede (1996b), who rightly emphasizes that *noein* for Aristotle is not ordinary thinking, but involves

   intellectually grasping something or having insight, in
   virtue of which we have true knowledge (p. 165).

30   With Ross in his *editio maior* (1961), but not his
   editio minor (1956), I start a new paragraph here.
   Likewise Smith, Barnes, Jannone-Barbotin. Another,
   less satisfactory way to signal Aristotle's change of
   subject is Theiler's: following Ritter, he puts angled
   brackets around 408b 18-29 and the whole of III 5
   to mark both as later insertions (by Aristotle himself). Siwek, by contrast, keeps a single paragraph
   on the grounds that 408b 18-29, so far from being
   a digression, is necessary to complete the proof that
   neither in its inferior *nor* its superior activities is the
   soul itself moved.

31   Two comments on this sentence. (1) Barnes
   replaced Smith's 'mind' with 'thought': 'But thought
   seems to be an independent substance implanted
   within us'. How *thought* could be an Aristotelian
   substance, of any kind, beggars belief. (2) Ross *ad
   loc*. rightly denies that this passage has to do with
   the doctrine of *GA* II 3, 736b 27-9, that '*nous* alone
   comes in from outside and it alone is divine'. The
   latter, as Caston (1999), 215-6, well argues, belongs
   with Aristotle's sexist biology, according to which an
   infant's form derives solely from the father, its matter
   from the mother. In the human case, the specific
   form contributed by the father is the power to think
   and reason. This power, which becomes actual as
   the infant grows up, is initially (as we shall see) *first*
   potentiality *nous*, no more. But for Aristotle it is as
   indestructible as the human race itself, though of
   course any individual's power to think and reason
   perishes when they do.

32 θεωρεῖν here is presumably the exercise of the intellectual understanding signified by νοεῖν. I preserve
the traditional translation 'contemplation', both
because it suggests a survey of results already won
(or in God's case, always known) rather than fresh
exploration, and from deference to the word's origin
(well traced by Nightingale) in the rites of viewing a
sacred spectacle. Barnes replaced Smith's 'the activity
of mind or intellectual apprehension' by 'thinking
and reflecting'.

33 In Hicks, Smith and Theiler the singular αὐτό
becomes the plural 'themselves'. The singular should
stand in the English because τὸ θεωρεῖν in mortal
humans is the intermittent exercise of the dispositional understanding called τὸ νοεῖν: they are one
and the same state at two levels of actuality.

34 Hicks renders διανοεῖσθαι as 'reasoning' here,
to keep 'thinking' from turning up on both sides
of the contrast—although 'thinking' was the word
he used for διανοεῖσθαι at 408b 14. Hamlyn leaves
us with an unexplained contrast between 'thought'
and 'thinking'. Barnes simply repeats 'thinking',
which in Smith's original stood in *contrast* to τὸ
νοεῖν καί τὸ θεωρεῖν. Ross *ad loc.*, surprised at the
way Aristotle groups τὸ διανοεῖσθαι with love and
hate as a feature of the composite rational animal,
rather than with τὸ νοεῖν alone, ventures an unlikely
explanation: 'Perhaps he does this because he thinks
of reasoning as getting at least one of its premises by
sense-perception'.

35 Alternatively, ἦν is the 'philosophical imperfect',
reaffirming what was said at 408b 25-7 (so Tricot,
Barbotin).

36 See n. 32 above.

37 My brackets in 'separate(d)' do not indicate alternative meanings of χωρίζεσθαι but alternative English expressions for a single meaning, as explained nn. 48 and 54 below.

38 In the light of the pairing τὸ νοεῖν καὶ τὸ φρονεῖν at III 3, 427a 18-19 and b 7-11, I take the two verbs γινώσκει τε ... καὶ φρονεῖ to contrast as theoretical to practical knowledge. Smith chooses 'think' for both φρονεῖν and νοεῖν, and proceeds to turn the chapter into a study of thinking instead of intellectual knowledge or understanding.

39 Ross in his summary switches here from 'thinking' to 'knowing' and then to 'reason' (p. 289).

40 'Understands' here is to be taken as 'has the capacity to understand', as the following sentence confirms.

41 The same claim was already made at *DA* II 5, 417a 21-7, though with the simpler examples of reading and writing; cf. my (2002), 48-9 with n. 59.

42 Alexander, *De anima libri mantissa* 110.4-6, with Zeller's compelling emendation Ἀριστοκλέους for Ἀριστοτέλους.

43 Aristotle posits a medium for taste and touch as well as for the distance senses. This enables him to argue that the heart within, not tongue or finger tip, is the organ of taste and touch. For detailed discussion I may refer to Burnyeat (1995) on Aristotle, followed by my (2001b) on Aquinas' insightful response.

44 For detailed discussion of light and the medium of vision in Aristotle, see my (1995), 422-7.

45 For defence of this claim, and rebuttal of the idea that Aristotle's cross-references witness to the chronology of his writing, see Burnyeat 2001a, chap. 5.

46   For a vigorous defence of the MSS ὥσπερ, excised
     by Ross, see Caston (1999), 205-7. The word is
     answered by καί at 430a 13.

47   Not 'matter for each thing of a given kind' (Wedin
     172).

48   ἐν τῇ ψυχῇ at line 13 parallels ἐν ἁπάσῃ τῇ φύσει
     at line 10 and so must be equally general: it *cannot*
     mean, what it is so often assumed to mean, e.g. by
     Ross (1961), 45, 'in the individual soul'; similarly
     without argument, alas, Aquinas, *in Ar. DA* Lectio X.
     The point is well argued by Caston (1999), 205-6.

49   I take the participial cause to be explanatory of the
     three features just listed: each rules out some type of
     potentiality (which in turn requires that χωριστός
     must mean 'separate', not 'separable'!). This speaks for
     'actuality' as the right translation of first instance for
     ἐνέργεια (cf. *Met.* Λ6, 1071b 19-20). Whether that
     actuality is best glossed as 'activity' is an issue that
     cannot be decided just on the basis of the exiguous
     text before us here. It is well to bear in mind *EN* VII
     14, 1154b: 'If there is some being whose nature is
     simple, the same mode of action will be continuously
     and in the highest degree pleasurable to it. Hence
     God enjoys everlastingly one pure pleasure. For there
     is actuality not only of change but also of *rest*, and
     pleasure consists rather in tranquillity than in change
     (οὐ γὰρ μόνον κινήσεώς ἐστιν ἐνέργεια ἀλλὰ καὶ
     ἀκινησίας, καὶ ἡδονὴ μᾶλλον ἐν ἠρεμίᾳ ἐστὶν ἢ ἐν
     κινήσει). (Tr. after Grant.)

50   It is hard to read 430 18's γάρ as a reason why this
     nous has the characteristics just listed, but it could
     instead give the author's reason for telling us about
     the characteristics it has: Denniston 60-61.

51 τιμιώτερον is expressly axiological; Wedin's 'superior' (p. 182) is insufficient.

52 I propose that ὅλως is well chosen to suggest ἐν τῷ ὅλῳ, 'in the universe at large', thereby lending point in this context to τὸ δ' αὐτό ... οὐ νοεῖ at 430a 19-22, which Ross *editio maior* (not *minor*) insists on bracketing. His grounds are given in his note *ad* III 5, 430a 19-22, and the follow-up note *ad* III 7, 431a 1-3: the words interrupt the discussion of the Active intellect in III 5, whereas III 7, where τὸ αὐτό ... χρόνῳ recur with a different sequel, is anyway a collection of scraps and there is no continuous sequence of thought to interrupt. The objection fails if the same words can be found relevant to III 5 as well. I suggest that 430a 22 ἀλλ' ... νοεῖ is precisely what does make them relevant to the Active Intellect.

53 I supply as subject here the only thing of which Aristotle could think the predicate true.

54 The aorist participle need no more imply a past act of separating than does the statement 'Marseilles is separated from Paris by a great distance'; Caston (1999), 208, aptly cites I 1, 403a 145, as a parallel where a past separation reading of χωρισθείς would make nonsense. Given the following exclusion of all but essential properties, the 'everything else' the divine *nous* is separated from must include, appropriately enough, separation from accidental properties.

55 Caston (1999), 213-5, proposes to translate ὅτι as 'that', not 'because', thereby diffusing centuries of controversy. Ingenious, but how, even in the heat of debate, could any competent student of Aristotle forget that anything which is παθητικός is thereby φθαρτικός and *vice versa*? The lack of memory testi-

fies to an important sense in which the life of the intellect is not *ours*, not part of our personal life. *Metaphysics* Λ 9 rather suggests that, to the extent that we became God for a while, we were the divine intellect understanding *itself* as that which understands all.

56   Here Smith and Barnes agree on 'without this, nothing thinks', which implies that no-one can draw up a shopping list without the aid of an eternal intellect.

57   The damage done by blinding light is often urged against my claim that for Aristotle normal seeing requires no material change in the organ (e.g. Lear, 114-115). The objection is analogous to Berkeley's notorious argument that, because blinding light produces pain in the mind, ordinary colours are also in the mind.

58   Brentano, p. 24, fulminating against Zeller.

59   Kurfess is a useful, manageably brief account of the long history of interpretations of *DA* III 5.

60   Thanks are owed (a) to the audiences with whom over the years I have shared thoughts and struggles on the topic of this lecture, at Ann Arbor, Berkeley, Budapest, Cambridge, Fribourg, Pittsburgh, Prague, and Princeton, (b) to Michael Frede (in his 1996a and elsewhere) and Victor Caston (in his 1999 paper) for their encouragement to join in the task of resurrecting a long neglected interpretation of *DA* III 5.

BIBLIOGRAPHY

Barbotin, E. See Jannone, A.

Barnes, J. See Smith, J.A.

Brentano, Franz. *The Psychology of Aristotle*. In Particular His Doctrine of the Active Intellect. With an Appendix Concerning the Activity of Aristotle's God. Edited and translated by Rolf George. Berkeley, Los Angeles & London: University of California Press, 1977

Burnyeat, M.F. 'How much happens when Aristotle sees red and hears middle C? Remarks on *De Anima* 2, 7–8', in paperback edition of *Essays on Aristotle's De Anima*, edd. Martha C. Nussbaum & Amélie Oksenberg Rorty (Oxford: Clarendon Press, 1995), 421–34

———. *A Map of Metaphysics Zeta*. Pittsburgh: Mathesis Publications, 2001a

———. 'Aquinas on "Spiritual Change" in Perception', in Dominik Perler ed., *Ancient and Medieval Theories of Intentionality* (Leiden, Boston and Cologne: Brill 2001b), 129–153

———. '*De Anima* II 5'. *Phronesis* 47 (2002), 1–64

———. 'On the Source of Burnet's Construal of *Apology* 30b 2-4 : A Correction'. *Journal of Hellenic Studies* 125 (2005), 139-142

Caston, Victor. 'Aristotle's Two Intellects: A Modest Proposal'. *Phronesis* 44 (1999), 199-227

———. 'The Spirit and the Letter: Aristotle on Perception'. In Ricardo Salles ed., *Metaphysics, Soul and Ethics: Themes from the Work of Richard Sorabji* (Oxford University Press, 2004), 245-320

Denniston, J.D. *The Greek Particles*. Oxford: Clarendon Press, 1934

Frede, Michael (1996a). 'La théorie aristotélicienne de l'intellect agent'. In Romeyer-Dherbey & Viano edd. (1999b), 377-390

———. 'Aristotle's Rationalism'. In Michael Frede & Gisela Striker edd., *Rationality in Greek Thought* (Clarendon Press: Oxford, 1996b), 157-173.

Grant, Sir Alexander. *The Ethics of Aristotle*. Illustrated with Essays and Notes. 2 vols. 4th edn., revised. London: Longman, Green & Co., 1885

Hadot, Pierre. 'La conception plotinienne de l'identité entre l'intellect et son objet: Plotin et le *De Anima* d'Aristote'. In Romeyer-Dherbey & Viano edd., 367-376

Hamlyn, D.W. *Aristotle's De Anima Books II and III* . Translated with Introduction and Notes. Clarendon Press: Oxford, 1968

Hicks, R.D. *Aristotle De Anima* with Translation, Introduction and Notes. Cambridge University Press, 1907

Jannone, A. *Aristote. De l'Âme*. Texte établi par A. Jannone; Traduction et Notes de E. Barbotin. Paris: Les Belles Lettres, 1966

Kurfess, Hans. *Zur Geschichte der Erklärung der aristotelischen Lehre vom sog. ΝΟΥΣ ΠΟΙΗΤΙΚΟΣ und ΠΑΘΗΤΙΚΟΣ*. Diss. Tübingen, 1911. Reprinted in *Greek and Roman Philosophy: A Fifty-Two Volume Reprint Set*, ed. Leonardo Tarán. New York & London: Garland Publishing, 1987

Lear, Jonathan. *Aristotle: the desire to understand*. Cambridge University Press, 1988

Nightingale, Andrea. *Spectacles of Truth in Classical Greek Philosophy: Theoria in its Cultural Context*. Cambridge University Press, 2004

Ritter, B. *Die Grundprincipien der arist. Seelenlehre.* Diss. Jena 1880

Rodis-Lewis, Geneviève. *Descartes: Meditationes de Prima Philosophia/ Méditations Métaphysiques.* Texte latin et traduction du Duc de Luynes. Introduction et notes. Paris: Vrin, 1967

Romeyer-Dherbey, Gilbert & Viano, Cristina, edd., *Corps et Âme: sur le De Anima d'Aristote.* Paris: Vrin, 1996

Ross, W.D. 'Smith, John Alexander (1863-1939)'. In L.G. Wickham ed., *Dictionary of National Biography 1931-1940* (Oxford University Press, 1949), 819-20

———. *Aristotelis De Anima.* Recognovit brevique adnotatione instruxit. Oxford University Press, 1956 [Ross *editio minor*]

———. *Aristotle De Anima.* Edited, with Introduction and Commentary. Oxford University Press, 1961 [Ross, *editio maior*]

———. *Aristotle, Metaphysica. The Works of Aristotle Translated into English under the Editorship of W.D. Ross.* Oxford: Clarendon Press, 1928.

Siwek, Paulus. *Aristotelis Tractatus De Anima.* Edidit, versione latina auxit, commentario illustravit. Collectio philosophica lateranensis. Rome: Desclée, 1965

Smith, J.A. 'On General Relative Clauses in Greek'. *Classical Review* 31 (1917), 69-71

———. *De Anima.* The Works of Aristotle translated under the general editorship of W.D. Ross. Vol. III. Oxford: Clarendon Press, 1931

Smith, J.A. & Jonathan Barnes. *Aristotle on the Soul.* The Complete Works of Aristotle. The revised Oxford Translation. 2 vols. Princeton University Press, 1984. [Based on the Greek text of Ross, *editio minor*]

Theiler, Willy. *Aristoteles. Über die Seele*. Übersetzt. Berlin: Akademie Verlag, 1959

Tricot, J. *Aristote De L'Âme*. Traduction nouvelle et notes. Paris: Vrin, 1947

Wedin, Michael. V. *Mind and Imagination in Aristotle*. New Haven & London: Yale University Press, 1988

THE AQUINAS LECTURES
Published by the Marquette University Press
Milwaukee WI 53201-3141

1. *St. Thomas and the Life of Learning.* John F. McCormick, S.J. (1937) ISBN 0-87462-101-1

2. *St. Thomas and the Gentiles.* Mortimer J. Adler (1938) ISBN 0-87462-102-X

3. *St. Thomas and the Greeks.* Anton C. Pegis (1939) ISBN 0-87462-103-8

4. *The Nature and Functions of Authority.* Yves Simon (1940) ISBN 0-87462-104-6

5. *St. Thomas and Analogy.* Gerald B. Phelan (1941) ISBN 0-87462-105-4

6. *St. Thomas and the Problem of Evil.* Jacques Maritain (1942) ISBN 0-87462-106-2

7. *Humanism and Theology.* Werner Jaeger (1943) ISBN 0-87462-107-0

8. *The Nature and Origins of Scientism.* John Wellmuth (1944) ISBN 0-87462-108-9

9. *Cicero in the Courtroom of St. Thomas Aquinas.* E.K. Rand (1945) ISBN 0-87462-109-7

10. *St. Thomas and Epistemology.* Louis-Marie Regis, O.P. (1946) ISBN 0-87462-110-0

11. *St. Thomas and the Greek Moralists.* Vernon J. Bourke (1947) ISBN 0-87462-111-9

12. *History of Philosophy and Philosophical Education.* Étienne Gilson (1947) ISBN 0-87462-112-7

13. *The Natural Desire for God.* William R. O'Connor (1948) ISBN 0-87462-113-5

14. *St. Thomas and the World State.* Robert M. Hutchins (1949) ISBN 0-87462-114-3

15. *Method in Metaphysics.* Robert J. Henle, S.J. (1950) ISBN 0-87462-115-1

16. *Wisdom and Love in St. Thomas Aquinas.* Étienne Gilson (1951) ISBN 0-87462-116-X

17. *The Good in Existential Metaphysics.* Elizabeth G. Salmon (1952) ISBN 0-87462-117-8

About the Aquinas Lecture Series

The Annual St. Thomas Aquinas Lecture Series began at Marquette University in the spring of 1937. Ideal for classroom use, library additions, or private collections, the Aquinas Lecture Series has received international acceptance by scholars, universities, and libraries. Hardbound in maroon cloth with gold stamped covers. Uniform style. Some reprints with soft covers. Complete set (ISBN 0-87462-150-X) receives a 40% discount. New standing orders receive a 30% discount. Regular reprinting keeps all volumes available.

Ordering information (purchase orders, checks, & major credit cards accepted):
   Marquette University Press
   Phone: (800) 247-6553
   Fax: (419) 281 6883
or order online at: http://www.mu.edu/mupress/

Editorial Address:
   Dr. Andrew Tallon, Director
   Marquette University Press
   P.O. Box 3141
   Milwaukee WI 53201-3141
Tel: (414) 288-1564 FAX: (414) 288-7813
email: andrew.tallon@marquette.edu

www.marquette.edu/mupress/

ISBN-13: 978-0-87462-175-4
ISBN-10: 0-87462-175-5